W9-CCH-725

# Memorial Day

# Memorial Day

by Geoffrey Scott

pictures by Peter E. Hanson

**Carolrhoda Books**
**Minneapolis**

Copyright © 1983 by CAROLRHODA BOOKS, INC.

All rights reserved. International copyright secured.
No part of this book may be reproduced in any form
whatsoever without permission in writing from the publisher
except for the inclusion of brief quotations in an acknowledged review.

Manufactured in the United States of America

LIBRARY OF CONGRESS CATALOGING IN PUBLICATION DATA

**Scott, Geoffrey,** 1952-
  Memorial Day.

  (A Carolrhoda on my own book)
  Summary: Explains why and how we celebrate
Memorial Day, the last Monday in May, a day set
aside to honor those who have fought and died
in the nation's wars.
    1. Memorial Day—Juvenile literature.
[1. Memorial Day. 2. Holidays] I. Hanson, Peter
(Peter E.), ill. II. Title. III. Series.
E642.S38   1983        394.2'684        83-1855
ISBN 0-87614-219-6 (lib. bdg.)

      3  4  5  6  7  8  9  10  90  89  88  87  86  85

Every year, on the last Monday in May,

we celebrate Memorial Day.

Memorial Day marks

the beginning of summer.

It is celebrated

all over the United States.

But why is it called Memorial Day?

What exactly are we celebrating?

Memorial Day has its beginnings
in the American Civil War.
Imagine you are living in the year 1863.
You are standing
at the edge of a hayfield.
Everything looks foggy
in the clouds of gunsmoke
that are rolling over the field.

Suddenly lines of blue-coated soldiers
charge through the smoke.
On the other side of the field
soldiers in gray coats stand waiting.
They are ready for the charge.
Rifle shots fill the air.
Cannons roar and spit out
flame and smoke.

Men scream and shout.

Gray and blue shapes fall to the ground.

Soon there are mounds of gray and blue

scattered across the field.

These are just some
of the many soldiers
who were wounded or killed
during the American Civil War.

In the Civil War
Americans fought Americans.
Soldiers from the southern states
fought soldiers from the northern states.

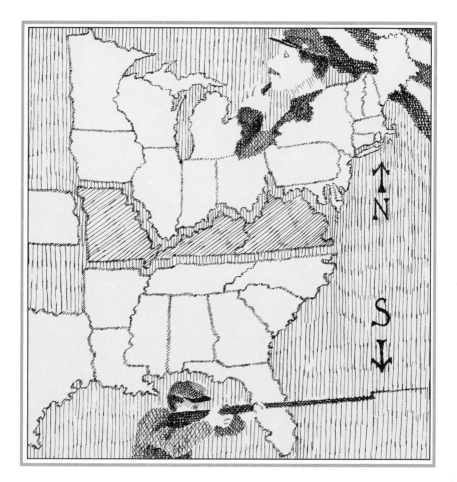

They were fighting
over whether or not the United States
would remain one country.
The southern soldiers wore gray.
The northern soldiers wore blue.
But what happened
if a man lived in New York
and his brother lived in Virginia?
Often brothers ended up
fighting against each other.
Fathers ended up
fighting against their sons.
Cousins fought cousins.
This made the Civil War
especially terrible.

The Civil War began in 1861.
It lasted for four long years.
Thousands of soldiers were killed
before it finally ended in 1865.

At last the soldiers could go home.
Of course they felt happy
that the war had ended,
but they felt other things too.

13

For one thing, they were worn out.

They had been fighting
for four long years.
Many of them had been injured.
Some had lost hands or arms.
Others had lost feet or legs.
They knew that their lives
were going to be very different
than they had been before the war.
Some soldiers had seen
their friends and relatives
die on the battlefields.
Others didn't find out
until they got home
that their brothers or fathers
had been killed in the war.

In the South,
where many of the battles
had taken place,

16

hundreds of soldiers arrived home
only to find that their homes
had been burned to the ground.

Henry C. Welles,

a druggist in Waterloo, New York,

watched the soldiers return

to his home town.

His feelings were mixed.

He felt happy that the war was over,
but he felt a lot of sadness too.
"We should do something," he said,
"something to honor the soldiers
who fought so hard for us
and something to honor those who died."
Henry Welles decided that Waterloo
should hold a celebration.
To honor those who had died in the war,
people would decorate their graves
with flowers and flags.
To honor the soldiers who had come home,
called veterans,
they could have a parade
on the way to the cemetery.

Welles talked to his friends.

Everyone thought he had a good idea.

So on May 5, 1866,

the people of Waterloo, New York,

honored the soldiers of the Civil War.

They called their celebration

Decoration Day.

Another man had an idea

very much like Welles's.

His name was General John A. Logan.

General Logan led a large group

of veterans from the North.

This group was called

the Grand Army of the Republic,

or G.A.R. for short.

General Logan issued an order

to all G.A.R. members.

He told them to decorate the graves

of northern soldiers.

He said they should do this

every year on May 30.

By 1868, Welles's Decoration Day
and the G.A.R. Decoration Day
had been joined.
The northern states all celebrated
Decoration Day on May 30.
Let's watch a small town
celebrate Decoration Day in 1878.
Decoration Day activities
began on May 29
in the one-room schoolhouse.
Students Sarah Goodhue
and Jonathan Freeborn
recited poems about the Civil War.

Then the class sang
"The Battle Hymn of the Republic."

Next Hiram Meeker gave a report
on Ulysses S. Grant's victory
at Vicksburg.

25

Then John Cottonwood spoke
to the students.

He was a veteran of the Civil War.
Cottonwood described the fighting
at the Battle of Gettysburg.
"The musket balls flying past my ears
sounded like huge mosquitoes.
I was plenty scared," he said.
Mr. Cottonwood explained
why everyone should remember
the dead soldiers.
"They died to keep the United States
united," he said.
At the end of his talk
the students sang
"The Star-Spangled Banner."
Then school was over for the day.

That evening families walked
to the local G.A.R. building.
They got ready
for the next day's celebration.
Children brought wildflowers
from the nearby fields.
Some people brought flowers
from their gardens.
Wives of G.A.R. members
tied the flowers into bouquets.
They put the bouquets
into big wooden tubs
filled with water.
This kept the flowers fresh
until the next morning.

The smell of food
floated out of the doors and windows.
Hams and turkeys were cooking inside;
so were huge pots of baked beans.
The food was for
the Decoration Day dinner.

Decoration Day began
just after sunrise.
The G.A.R. members
raised the American flag.
To honor the dead,
they raised it only halfway
up the flagpole.

Then the veterans
had their picture taken
near the flag.
Doc Renville and William Scott
wore their battered blue army caps.

The Stearn brothers wore G.A.R. emblems
on their black felt hats.
Lansford Fillmore wore the medals
he had won
at the Battle of Fort Donelson.

Then it was time for the veterans
to lead the parade.
A fife, a drum, and a small brass band
followed them.
The townspeople brought up the rear.
They all marched to the town cemetery.
Everyone carried bouquets of flowers
and small American flags.
The band played softly.
It was a quiet, thoughtful parade.
People thought about the dead soldiers.
They thought about veterans
who had been wounded,
like Lansford Fillmore,
who had lost one leg.

At the cemetery, women and children
decorated the graves.
They placed a flag
and some flowers on each one.
They straightened and cleaned
the cast iron G.A.R. emblems
that decorated many of the graves.
Then Pastor Mower said a prayer.
Six G.A.R. men fired their rifles
three times into the air
as a salute to the dead soldiers.
Finally someone played "Taps"
on the bugle.

Then everyone marched back
to the G.A.R. building.
Soon the big supper was served.
People ate and talked.
The Wright sisters talked
about their brother and father.
"Father died at Fredericksburg,

fighting for the South," Emma said.

"And Benjamin fell outside Richmond.

He fought for the North," said Edith.

The sisters felt sad,

but they were thankful for peace.

It was a sad and a happy day.

It was Decoration Day, 1878.

Not long after this, in 1882,
the G.A.R. changed the name of
"Decoration" Day
to "Memorial" Day.
The G.A.R. thought it would be better
to remember the dead from all wars,
not just the Civil War.
They wanted the remembering
to be as important
as the decorating.
By this time
Decoration Day was a legal holiday
in many northern states,
but southern states
did not celebrate Decoration Day.

They did have a holiday like it,

but the date of that holiday

was different in every southern state.

It wasn't until 1971

that Memorial Day was declared

a national holiday by President Nixon.

America has fought in many wars
since the Civil War.
We have many more
dead soldiers to remember
on Memorial Day,
but many of our celebrations
are not so different
from those in the 1800s.
Many towns still have parades.
Veterans march in them
and military bands play.
Children,
especially Boy Scouts and Girl Scouts,
decorate soldiers' graves.

43

Soldiers at army bases
fire their rifles into the air.

Navy sailors throw flowers
into the ocean.
That is their way
of honoring dead sailors.

Many people have picnics
and family gatherings.
Some of our celebrations
have changed, though.
Today we often remember
all of our dead relatives
on Memorial Day,
even if they were not soldiers.
Another change is the date.
Memorial Day no longer
always falls on May 30.
In 1971 it was moved
to the last Monday in May,
which is when most states
now celebrate Memorial Day.

But even though the name and date
of the holiday have changed,
our reasons for celebrating it
remain much the same.
Memorial Day is still a day
on which we celebrate peace
and remember those
who have died in wars.

OCT 0 5 1988

J394.2684    Scott, Geoffrey, 1952-
             Memorial Day

             R00559 71507

795

VC

11 KIRKWOOD
ATLANTA-FULTON PUBLIC LIBRARY